Already Alive

Sydney Osborn

Copyright © 2013 Sydney Osborn

All rights reserved.

ISBN: 0615984584
ISBN-13: 9780615984582

Fame is for the dead; I'm just looking to be heard.

CONTENTS

	Acknowledgments	1
1	Ripples	3
2	Running Out of Time	4
3	Bittersweet Farewell	5
4	Recovery	6
5	Thanks for the Help	7
6	Sad Robots	8
7	Mixing Fate and Family	9
8	Through the Gates of Hell	10
9	Stolen Sunrise	12
10	No Flash Photography, Please	13
11	A Crack in the Sidewalk	14
12	A Slayer's Demise	15
13	Soft Spoken	16
14	Belonging	17
15	Fourth Story Windowsill	18
16	My Soldier, My Hero, My Love	19
17	Buried Alive	20
18	Departure	22
19	Flier	23
20	City of Curtain	24

21	Goodbye Sweet Alaska	26
22	New Years	27
23	Girl in the White City	28
24	Natural Beauty	30
25	Reflections of Anig	31
26	Odd One Out	32
27	New Kid	33
28	The Tunnel's Train of Thought	35
29	Stand Up or Give Up	36
30	Ashes	37
31	Extinguished	38
32	Breaking Boundaries	39
33	The End	40
34	Dearest Life	41

ACKNOWLEDGMENTS

To those who think that I can, and those who think that I cannot, I thank you for your constant inspiration.

Ripples

You are hardly a speck in this universe; a speck the size of stars and you're still merely dust. So the size of your words uttered but once into this crowded barren plane of space and time will mean nearly nothing to those who came before and will surely come afterwards. But for today, how do these murmurs affect those floating on about you? Though you have your six inches of space, there are billions nearby who await those words to fall upon their ears. Never deaf nor blind to the injustice you've portrayed with a single word. But in time, I suppose, that word will just float away, becoming less than dust in the days to come; less than you and I. These blind words wisp away and become echoes in the universe. But where might they resonate?

Running Out of Time

life's a clock hung on the wall
ticking chimes of impatience
wondering how far it has to fall

a short life lived from eight feet tall
reporting on its evidence
life's a clock hung on the wall

a sad life lived against the wall
all chances come in coincidence
wondering how far it has to fall

a big life lived from 3 feet small
there are few I could convince
life's a clock hung on the wall

no life lived according to protocol
drab and lonely by convenience
wondering how far it has to fall

life ticks by after all
ticking chimes of impatience
life's a clock hung on the wall
wondering how far it has to fall

Bittersweet Farewell

The wrinkles on her fingers
Echo like rings on a tree
Chopped down past it's prime.
It had lived in its time.

And the smile on her face
Speaks volumes from the past.
Libraries of wisdom
Whose memories can't last.

And the voice whispering softly
Seems to whither as it goes,
Humming solemn lullabies
Of bittersweet farewell.

Recovery

Every story has its ending.
Everything built must fall apart.
What is broken is unbending.
Success is only for the strong at heart.
A sense of doom which is impending;
Every ending has its start.

Not so feeble minded;
Only faint at heart.
My aches begin their mending;
I watch as you depart.

Something above comprehending.
My love for you remains,
Unending.

Thanks for the Help

Lost in endless time and space.
Questions from the past;
Reminded of memories long repressed.
To be alone in a world of billions.
An offer of help which won't assist.
Therapies cause confusion and hatred.
Far from intoxicated,
But the circle grows larger by one.
A daunting empty blackboard
As scratches in it quickly deepen
With just the eyes that wander towards her.

No chip for I am not sober,
No medals for I am not clean.
Should I squalor in the filth I call my own?
Another day spent wasting away a dream.
A leap backwards,
As a brave step toward the finish
Slowly recedes.

I'm still a disability.

Sad Robots

Just comply with life,
Because we're all too afraid to object where it counts.
We fear rejection and judgment.
We fear fear itself.
We live inside our little boxes,
Most of us are sealed tightly inside,
And though we each have knives
to let ourselves outside,
Nobody dares defy the constraint of our daily lives.
It seems that those who dare stand out,
Are always pushed aside.

Mixing Fate and Family

Who knew it could flourish and bloom?
Who saw it coming
Much too soon?
How, those years ago,
Could they imagine
The colors would show.

Passing moons and mistakes;
A wet code welcomes a crack in the shell.
A hard shell broken
By flow of emotion,
An inundation is to pursue.

And so the bud becomes a sprout,
The sprout a glorious blossom;
A crack in the sidewalk,
A line on a map.

A scar in the past
Will never be the same;
The future is ours
To mangle and tame.

Through the Gates of Hell

Liberation is almost impossible, that's why it's only for the seldom strongly-willed individual.

I've recently learned that freedom comes at a high cost.
Though, as a nation we're supposedly free,
We're locked behind secrets individually.

Like biking up a hill,
The hardest part is to keep them.
Your knees grow weak and your legs become sore.
You're still at the bottom,
But aching for more.

As you climb towards the summit,
You wonder what's in store.
Will your sore legs betray you?
Will you crash to the floor?

As the bruises and bumps
Multiply on your thighs,
The burning sensation just presses you on
And the fear in your heart ignites flames as you depart.

The summit is within reach
But your knees have gone weak.
The strength is within you,
To press on and continue.

And though the top hurts like hell,
Your uphill battle is behind you.
And downhill from here,
Your tracks will remind you
That trailblazing isn't easy,
But your past can't define you.

And as you speed towards the finish,
Gleaming faces you'll see;
They cheered you on the whole time,
And they always believed.

I did great things before, and now that I'm free,
You'll see the good I can do
And how great I can be.

Stolen Sunrise

I have clouds of sulfur in my eyes
That cloud my truth and give me lies.
In my bed awake at night,
I lie for hours frozen in fright.
He lurks behind my bed,
Runs crazy nightmares through my head.
He keeps me up and I don't sleep,
Because behind every corner there's a creep.
The noise of the heater cracking at dawn
Peels my eyes from where they belong.
A sudden jolt reminds me I'm alive,
But in my dreams I don't survive.

Sydney Osborn

No Flash Photography, Please.

The way they look at me you'd guess I was deformed
Or something.
Maybe just ashamed;
We know that one's true.
And how about that hair?
Or the way she gasps for air?
I wonder why she's purple.
Her blood runs to flee the circle.

Three months later and she's home
For better or worse
The outsiders never know.

Don't look!
No sense in remembering.

Flashes! Flashes!
We all fall
Down.

A Crack in the Sidewalk

I don't view this place as beautiful anymore. The summer hid all the cracks in the sidewalk, but with the start of winter they came back. All my memories are paved over; all the good ones fade to black.

Pages turn- I can't look back.
It seems that the dark is all I see;
Starved of air and sanity.
I remember this place
From back when I played:
Glad I didn't stay
To watch the laughter fade.

The years have passed and spring is marked by the cracks in the sidewalk filling with grass.

The shards of the broken
Gnaw at my feet.
Naked, I feel;
Exposed to new heat.
And though the chill from the winter air is gone,
The buds have not blistered
With the breath of a new dawn.

A Slayer's Demise

A red rage hides
Behind my dull eyes.
I hope you perish.
Fall into the depths of hell,
Along with all your lies.
Bury yourself deep,
Where only grotesque creatures sleep.
Burn,
And in ashes they'll reap.
Until I see those ashes,
I won't believe.

And in a coffin made for two
Only one will sleep.
Because I'd rather die alone
Than be within your reach.

Soft Spoken

I don't feel like I'm dying,
I feel like I'm dead.
I'm no longer bleeding,
I've already bled.
I beg you; release me
From what I've already said.

Belonging

Slanting through silence.
Blankly staring at the shadow across your blanket.
Cast upon by blinds,
The daunting jail cell lines.

Remaining but a mystery,
All we've got is history,
And I can't imagine being much happier than that.

Cold rocks form welts where mouths should reside.
Cells and walls alike will die.
Lost within a purple studded nightmare;
Pitch black with your diamonds of plum.

Slow and uneven pace;
A struggle but not a race.
That is where the box should be;
Nothing there for us to see.

A studded neck brace
Blurring fine lines.
A beaten porcelain face,
Slurring all but rhymes.

The tail of your coat whisks away.
Your fingertips whisper farewell.
Wheels resume their spinning.
How long should I stand in one place?

Fourth Story Windowsill

A hundred days in May
And you flew a hundred miles
Just to get away.

Maybe there are miles between
But we both know where we've been.
Peel back the screen,
Open the window.
Let air revive our hollow lungs.

Soothe passion's fever in the wind,
Let life caress our sweaty skin.

Scream at the skies,
As they dim
In our eyes.

Stare far and wide;
See the world begin.

Breathing youth,
I feel like a kid.

Forever and a day-
Let the games begin.

My Soldier, My Hero, My Love

My soldier
Stand tall
Even if the world seems big,
Even if you may feel small.
Stand tall, brave soldier.
The battles will soon be over.

My hero,
Stay near.
Even while you stand thousands of miles away.
Even if the day never comes,
Stay near, hero.
I need you here.

My love,
Fight bravely.
Stand as though there are no winds against you.
Even if you begin to fall,
Expect to see me there,
I'll catch you.
Fight bravely, love.
You will be home soon.

Buried Alive

The magic's gone
He stuck a knife through his ear;
He pulled a rabbit from his hat.
Stole your ring,
And gave it back.

A stare or two from across the room,
The truth is hidden in the angles.

And now the car that's driving past,
Contains breathing hearts
That won't wave back.

Staring here,
From the magicians booth;
Left alone:
A table set for two.

The magic words,
And in a poof,
The car is gone,
And so are you.

Magic shows:
The world flashed before my eyes,
But he was blind;
He can't see magic from behind.

The angle shows the magic's gone,
The wind bites sharply at the dawn;
Awaiting the white steed that will never come.
The night is darkest before the sun.

Hidden beneath the wintry skies,
On a dangerous corner is where she lies.
Completely hidden from bright lights;
Only visible through blind eyes.

And while the light inside slowly dies,
Her skin is scarred by kind frostbite.

Departure

Tears feel warm
Against cold skin
But my cheeks feel warm
Where your hands have been.

You whisper "Don't forget,"
As you wave goodbye.
You leave to board that jet,
But my broken wings won't fly.

A sad scrap mutters
"See You Soon"
to make a sad heart flutter?
Or possibly a clue?

And as winds whip and whistle.
I walk a lonely road.
Memories of times never forgotten.
A place that I call home.
A gentle face to call my own.

I may be lonely, but I'll never be alone.

Flier

They're looking up at me,
Just a thousand feet.
I'm balanced precariously
With no chance for retreat.

As I begin to sink
The wind is my savior;
Wiping at my lashes,
Gripping my last breath.
A force before she crashes.

The crowd surrenders.
I'm left standing in the street.
A life of foreseen benders
Ends with my last defeat.

City of Curtain

City of curtain,
Walls of blue,
Things have changed here
With the loss of you.
The city is grey now;
Lost all of its hue.

Can't quite find words to express
The sadness, chaos,
And duress.

The cruelty shown
Upon your wake,
You left curtain
To seek your fate.

And now the city-
Black and blue,
Painted sorrow;
Tried and true.

Tested citizens
Failed their trust
Once inhabited-
Filled with dust.

Flipped the hourglass,
Fine grains pass.
Counting down
To lay with grass.

And grow may the sprouts of all you have done,
Your remains but flowers
Beneath a grey sun.

Try as you might,
None shall pass.
Curtains conceal
The looking glass.

All that is beyond,
And all that have passed
Curtains conceal
The looking glass.

The flame in the heavens
Has fizzled at last.
Curtains conceal
The looking glass.

Goodbye Sweet Alaska

Never a second chance,
Or a clear reason why,
and through my pleading calls
All that answered was goodbye.

Before we ever met,
You were severed from my heart.
Your little bloodied body
Still lies on the floor.

The letters you'll never receive
And the plans that will never be played
Still race around my mind
As I realize I'm enslaved.

I said he'd be good,
For all that you are,
But it looks like I lied from the start.
And now you aren't.

Goodbye, sweet Alaska.
Your letters end with me.
Those kind letters to Alaska
Will never be set free.

The man who took you from me
Will never be caught
Because it's not a crime
To lose your train of thought.

New Years

Who are we to judge those to come before us?
A wilder wisdom,
Though we've grown.
With each advancement
Less is known.

Never breathe to inhale;
Inhale to have life stolen
If only for a moment.
For these are how to measure the years.
Not for what we've discovered.
Not for how far we've come.
For each time we find material,
Another wisdom dies.

Those these eyes can't recognize
All to come before,
We find that we materialize
All that we stand for.

A head above water will surely drown
A star from the heavens;
A meteor comes down.
Every shining, invented light
From every single town
Falls upon the sticks and stones
To curse what we have found.

Don't let us rejoice at each newly found;
Let us find each other.
Let us sleep just one more night
In only silent sound.

Girl in the White City

She walked as if she'd never cared a day in her life.
She carried a slow contemptuous smile on her face.
Her hair fell in random waves across her shoulders and down her back, and kissed the wind that couldn't quite penetrate her leather jacket.

She had sex and hatred in her gray eyes.
She was a killer.
That is not to say that she had killed before, but rather that she could, and that she might.

Her anger was intoxicating.
She lusted for pain and the thrill of danger.

Her footsteps fell heavy on the cracked pavement.
Her black boots appeared matte and tattered on the burning asphalt.
She wore jeans that hugged her thighs.
She was tall and thin, but not the girl anyone envied in high school.

She carried her keychain carelessly around her ring finger.
The keys clanged together and the noise rang through the lot.
She swung them melodically in her hand as she walked.

The sight of her was mesmerizing.
She captured all the senses.
The smell of her leather jacket and the sound of her keys danced in the air and wrapped me in her virtue.
The back and fourth motion of her hair matched her keychain and was interrupted by even the slightest wind.

This was her weakness.
The wind disturbed the pattern she carried and it filled me with hatred.

My hatred was different than hers. She held a silent hatred in her gray eyes.
My hatred had passion and fire behind it.
I wanted to take her hatred and replace it with mine.

I needed to see if there were flecks of blue despair in those gray eyes.
I needed to know if there was hazel passion or green lust.
I needed to be close- to smell the leather and the hatred she wore.
I couldn't let her remain this passionless soul.
I ached to give her something: terror, excitement, sorrow...
These emotions were missing from her steady waltz.

I am the wind today.
I will fluster her hair and dance across her lashes.
I will feel the specks of green and blue and hazel.

Today I will penetrate that leather jacket.
I will show her that she could kill, but she won't.
I will make her see a day when she cares for life.
And then I'll take it all away.

Natural Beauty

Beautiful and billowing,
Constantly falling,
Infinitely.

As one droplet strays
Beauty falls from a porcelain face.
The drop evaporates,
But the beauty stays.

Take this handkerchief,
Just in case.
And don't be afraid;
If you find yourself drowning,
I'll always keep you safe.

Reflections of Anig

You were all I see,
All I ever cared for,
Now all I can tell you,
Is R-I-P.

I loved your smile,
Your laugh,
Your eyes.
I loved the way you sleep at night.
I loved how I could always rely
On the one who always wanted to die.
Your beauty surpasses all that I know,
So let it be,
My friend or foe.
If you love it,
Let it go.

Odd One Out

Different is bad
Everyone should be the same.
They say you're imperfect
If you can't fit into their frame.
They say if you step outside the boundaries they've made,
You are allowed nothing but shame.
Look at this stellar hell you've come to create.
Good luck living through your karma-studded fate.
This world is filled with nothing but hate.

Sydney Osborn

New Kid

You can still see the sunshine through closed eyes.
Squeeze them tightly;
Find there's no place to hide.
Maybe life is easy on the brighter side.

Alone behind bars;
A stomach filled with only scars.
A neck encircled by restraint,
What I'd give for light of day.

One more night of frolic and play,
From my child I run astray.
A truth I'd never think to face-
Now I sit alone-
Replaced.

The Tunnel's Train of Thought

I've left the light behind,
Ran fifteen feet into the depths of my own mind.
Kept my feet moving without my eyes to guide them.
Kept my mind moving
Without the light to blind them.

I kept the switch set to off,
Traveling uncharted trails
Worn by feet before,
But my mind shall be the first.
A virgin to these revolutionary thoughts.
Never a glimmer in the thick of it.
Hope is all that remains
As thoughts consume my brain.
When vision is no longer a factor,
The mind can trail off to wonderful places.

Entering the tunnel,
I should have slowed my pace.
I entered the darkest part of the race.
I picked up my feet,
With ambition I ran towards the darkness.
As hope was taken to a climax I began to slow.
Why should I not embrace the darkness,
Why not embrace the trail of thought?

Though the darkness may consume me,
Sure I may be covered in a black abyss,
But these are welcomed attributes of a freed mind.
Miles pass;
While my brain says to give up,
Hope keeps telling me to try.

Sydney Osborn

Left and right are what I know for sure to be true.
Up or down may never again show themselves to the shame of daylight.
Thoughts, far from material;
They are what I have.
In one hand I hold a flashlight-
What a trivial thing.
I travel countless blackened miles,
What justice will this talisman bring?

Submerged in darkness,
I am running.
I pray I never see the light,
But darkness subsides to daytime,
The tiny light ahead heeds to the pitter-patter of my own two feet.
I beat the abyss,
But I feel only defeat.
An unwelcome entrance,
Or a hasty retreat?

Stand Up or Give Up

Somebody needs to do something.
How about you?
Somebody needs to stop this.
Who?
Will you wait for *Someone*
To do it for you?

Shouldn't we find Someone?
Maybe someday?
Will someone find *someday*?
Whenever that might be...

I guess we're getting nowhere,
Since no one will step up.
I guess we'll just waste our days,
Waiting on someone else.

I won't be the one waiting around,
I can do this for myself.
I'll change the world,
While you sit and wait
For 'Someone' to come to town.

Ashes

Burn behind my wrath.
Never cross my path,
For when I come near
All that lives will sear.

I never was the gentle kind;
Dancing in ferocious winds.
Not a sympathetic mind;
Never blamed for my sins.

Maybe had I been punished-
Banished with thick foam,
I could've been extinguished;
Not so free to roam.

But winds persisted,
And oxygen fed my blaze.
Now the world is blistered
With my smoky haze.

The crimes of humans inflamed
With hues of orange and blue.
Though they may be hidden,
The memories remain askew.

The dangers of a hidden past,
Ashes can't hide all.
The memories sneak up fast,
And in ashes you shall fall.

Extinguished

Wash the flame,
It cleanses my breath.
Heat sears my dusty throat.
I swallow deeply to forget the pain.
It follows into my gut.
I lose the will to continue as my insides are swiftly burned away.

Hell resides within my sides.
Every organ slowly dies.
My heart's constant fire is burned away with a more literal flame.
My body's metronome no longer ticks.
What is left is buried below the earth,
Covered by beauty, in foliage and sticks.

Breaking Boundaries

Though I have not found
A single strand
To hell I am bound.
Destined to chase the soulless,
Grasping to their tails,
I head down a path,
Reaped by only trolls.
To saunter down a path
Still virgin to new souls,
And dance upon a memory-
Fleeting as it unfolds.

Down a path not made for skipping,
Along a river not made for stones.
Red walls covered high
In naked bars and bones.

And behind a web is spun
To entangle all but one.
Each strand takes another captive,
Forever things are trapped in
The sickly wall of souls.

If a soul were to escape
The spider loses sleep.
The web of souls is much too weak-
The captor stays awake.

And though no dawn will ever break,
The morning brings a wary eye.
The spider made a huge mistake;
The walls are now alive.

The End

Get me out of here,
Take me anywhere but here.
Kill me inside.
Kill my vision;
Make me blind.
Call my bluff,
Catch my drift.
Enough is enough.

This is it.

Dearest Life

I'm dying. Slowly, every single day, I will die. Before I sleep I will kiss today goodbye. "Dearest life, I've lived you for but a day. I valued all that you brought me in these 24 hours. Goodnight and goodbye. "

I'm dying. Slowly, every week, I will die. Before Monday, I will kiss my week goodbye. "Dearest life, I've experienced you for but a week. I valued all the progress I've made. The farther I traveled in this life the more I've come to value it. Goodnight and goodbye."

I'm dying. Slowly, every year, I will die. Before the first, I will kiss my year goodbye. "Dearest life, I've grown through you for but a single year. I valued the successes I've found, as well as the struggles I've faced. The closer the end approached, the faster I worked, the happier I learned to become. Goodnight and goodbye."

I'm dying. Slowly, in this lifetime, I will die. Before the last, I will kiss my days, weeks, and years goodbye. "Dearest life, I have valued you for but a short lifetime. I valued each moment, whether it be one of heartbreak or of bliss. Though I never knew which moment would be my last, I learned to value each day. Each day I lived as if it were my last; each night I kissed my life goodbye. This life was made up of each last day. Goodnight and goodbye."

On our very last day, of the very last week, of the very last year, what will matter? As these moments flash before your eyes, who will you see? What memories will they bring? And most importantly, *will you be happy?*

Already Alive

A Note from the Author

Everyone has something in their past they're not proud of. But one of the many beautiful things about humanity is that you wouldn't know it to just look at somebody. You can't tell by looking at someone that they've ever suffered any harm.
You would think that this veil of ignorance would be a bad thing, but instead it is infinitely beneficial because it allows us to look past the scars of our past to a new day that is brighter and more beautiful than the day before.
I've learned from my past, but my past will never own me.

www.ingramcontent.com/pod-product-compliance
Lightning Source LLC
Chambersburg PA
CBHW060223050426
42446CB00013B/3147